AF333872

BRIEFCASE

David Gene Fowler

Wings Press
Houston

Cover photograph by unknown photographer
at San Francisco production

ISBN 0-930324-15-3
©1979 Wings Press
Printed in the U.S.A.

Wings Press
P.O. Box 25296
Houston, TX 77005

Production History of "Brief Case"

The premiere of BRIEF CASE occurred at the church in Austin, Texas in June, 1976. It was directed by the author with the following cast:

HANCE .... Brian Papageorge
BABYDOLL .... Nina Martin
MR. DOLL .... Charles Gruber
MRS. DOLL .... Sarah Bolz

Set art by Rick Turner and Robin Gaynes

The second production took place at Studio Eremos in San Francisco in June, 1977. It was directed by Ruthanne Ramm with the following cast:

HANCE .... Max Diamond
BABYDOLL .... Meg Mettler
MR. DOLL .... Hesh Rosen
MRS. DOLL .... Lisa Stranger

The Studio Eremos production was subsequently broadcast on Channel 6 cable television, San Francisco, in July, 1977.

A third production occurred at Interart Studio, Austin, in June, 1978. It was directed by Susan Bright with the following cast:

HANCE .... Danny O'Dell
BABYDOLL .... Sallie Jacque
MR. DOLL .... Charles Gruber
MRS. DOLL .... Karen Krause

Lighting for this production was provided by Heinz Schulze

From the first production
Photo by Rick Turner

Scene: a living room in the United States. Couch, tv set, etc. BABYDOLL *wears houserobe, perhaps hair curlers, etc.* HANCE *enters, wearing underwear (any style, suggest boxer shorts) and from waistline to neck a standard white business shirt and tie are painted on his body or he simply wears actual same. He wears hat and sunglasses which he takes off. Also takes off imaginary suitcoat, hangs it up.*

HANCE: Babydoll! It's me! Your husband! Hance! Home from Another Day at the Office!

BABYDOLL: *(runs to him.)* Hance! Darling! *(they embrace.)*

HANCE: *(throws down briefcase, sits down in big chair or couch)* I want a bottle of pop! BABYDOLL *scurries away.)* Jesus, what a day. (BABYDOLL *returns, hands* HANCE *bottle of Pop, perhaps red Nehi.)*

BABYDOLL: Pop! *(curtsies, large artificial smile.)*

HANCE: Pop! *(drinks)*

BABYDOLL: Pop! *(curtsies, large artificial smile.)*

HANCE: Pop! *(drinks, they both laugh.)* I wanna read the paper!
(BABYDOLL *scurries away to get the paper, she returns, hands paper to* HANCE, *he begins to read.)*

BABYDOLL: Oh Hance! How wonderful! How luscious! *(she kisses him, mussing up the paper and spilling his Nehi.)* Oh Precious! Oh Rapture!

HANCE: *(stands. strikes photographic pose.)* With purrrfect freedom fit, no riding-up and no ugly elastic marks!

BABYDOLL: Oh Hance! Oh Marvelous! Oh Exquisite! Oh Divine!

HANCE: As Natural as your Own Skin! Loose cling snug support!

BABYDOLL: Oh Hance! Oh Splendor! Oh! Lights! Camera! Oh Ecstasy! Oh Photograph!

HANCE: Yes! It is quite exciting. *(sits back down.)* I wanna watch tv!

(BABYDOLL *scurries over and turns on television, without sound. Music provided by another source. Upbeat.)*

BABYDOLL: Come on Hance! Dance with me!

HANCE: Not now Babydoll. I've had a hard day.

BABYDOLL: Oh come on Hancie! Just one dance—you're not too tired! *(she moves more provocatively.)* Come on! It's FUN!

HANCE: *(divided interest between tv and* BABYDOLL.*)* No, not now. Really BD, I'm beat. This is a really good program. What is it?

BABYDOLL: *(moves more provocatively)* Oh come on Hance! Let's dance! Hey Soldier, I've got your number! Come on! You'll like it! Come on! Get on your feet and feel the beat!

HANCE: *(giving in)* Oh okay. *(they dance cheek to cheek.)* Hey yeah. This is really kinda neat!

BABYDOLL: OOoooooooh! *(laughs)*

HANCE: Hheeeeeyy! *(laughs) (dance undergoes gradual transformation from waltzy box-step to eventual bopping, twisting, shaking, laughing, singing, etc.)*

BABYDOLL: Go Hance! Go man go!

HANCE: Hey Babydoll! Move out! Shake it!

BABYDOLL: Weeeeeee! Oooh!! OOooh! Weeeee!

HANCE: Ho! Hi! Ha! Hee! Hooo! *(stops dancing)* MY NAME IS HANCE AND THAT'S SHORT FOR HANDSOME!

BABYDOLL: MY NAME IS BABYDOLL AND THAT'S SHORT FOR EVE! MY DADDY OWNS HISTORY!

HANCE: I always said we should spend more time with your parents.

BABYDOLL: What? With you in your underwear?! Are you kidding?

HANCE: Well of course with me in my underwear. I mean a guy's gotta make a living.

BABYDOLL: But Hance that's just not the kind of thing you tell your parents. "What does your husband do dear?" "Oh he's an underwear modeler mother." I can see it now.

HANCE: You mean they don't know?

BABYDOLL: Of course not. Do your parents know?

HANCE: Well of course. They have all my catalogues bound in gold leaf editions. They leave some of the best ones on the coffee table to show off to their friends. To them I am a very successful young professional.

BABYDOLL: *(laughs)* PHOTOGRAPH!

*(*HANCE *gets down on all fours and sniffs around like a dog.)*

BABYDOLL: PHOTOGRAPH!

*(*HANCE *jumps up and acts like he is riding a horse and waving a big cowboy hat.)*

BABYDOLL: PHOTOGRAPH!

*(*HANCE *assumes gorilla persona. He beats his chest, cries out, pops the elastic band of his underwear, cries out, lurks around the room, cries out, picks up* BABYDOLL *who is laughing hysterically, cries out, he holds her perpendicular to himself, and dances soft shoe number to tv music.* BABYDOLL *laughs hysterically, muttering "Photograph" while flailing her arms and legs. Both laughing, they collapse on couch. Begin wrestling, giggling, exhausted, roll to silent point.* BABYDOLL *gets up, straightens herself.)*

BABYDOLL: Photograph! Shit, Hance. You know what you are? You're a weirdo!

HANCE: *(stands, adjusts his underwear, circles her while speaking.)* May I remind you of how our romance began, my dear wife? If memory serves correctly you saw my "international" lay-out in the spring-summer, 1972 edition of Sears and Roebuck's catalogue. The ad said: "JET-SET Briefs. For the guy who's got it and for the guy who wants to get it." There were several pages of great shots of me standing in front of various wonders of the world in daring multi-colored jet-sets. You said that when you saw me reclining provocatively in a pair of "Shangri-la blue mist" jet-sets in front of the Etruscan Mother Goddess you told yourself, "That's the man I'm going to marry." You somehow found out who I was and began writing me letters. I evaded you at first—I was skeptical as to whether or not you truly appreciated the art of underwear modeling. For months I thought you were just an impressionable young girl squealing through some pop fad or latest craze. But when you began to exhibit dangerous signs of irreparable heartbreak I decided I had better check you out. I really thought you were going to take some desperate action, maybe even harm yourself unless I contacted you. And I sure didn't want that on my conscience. So, I called you. . . *(*BABYDOLL *getting angry,* HANCE, *circling her, pacing).* . . And another thing, Babydoll, if your parents don't know I'm an underwear modeler, then what did they think when I showed up at the wedding not wearing any pants?

BABYDOLL: I told them the tuxedo rental shop messed up your pants and couldn't get them fixed in time. They were shocked of course and embarrassed but I guess they just finally got over it. I mean, you did have on a tux coat and a nice white shirt and tie. . .You know, come to think of it my Aunt Ethel said that she really did admire your jet black silk of the night Big Boy Boxer Shorts.

HANCE: Gee. Really? Really? Gee.

BABYDOLL: Anyway that's why I've only let you meet my parents that one time. They think you're a travelling meat buyer for a big food company based in Atlanta.

HANCE: Gimme a break, Babydoll. I mean I'm practically like a celebrity and you won't even tell your parents.

BABYDOLL: Well I just don't see any reason to upset them. And it would upset them terribly. They just wouldn't know how to handle it. . .Why do you think my father kept asking you about the meat business all through the reception?

HANCE: I just assumed that's what he called the underwear modeling business. Jesus, a man breaks his back all day, five days a week, 48 weeks a year, and his wife is ashamed of him!

BABYDOLL: I'm not ashamed of you Hancie. But you must admit, most men do wear pants when they're working.

HANCE: So what? What does a pair of pants have to do with it? Besides, a few minutes ago, you thought underwear modeling was exciting. What's gotten into you?

BABYDOLL: I don't know Hance. Maybe I'm just maturing. It's all so bizarre.

HANCE: Bizarre? There's nothing 'bizarre' about underwear. Underwear is basic, fundamental. Almost everyone wears underwear. The President wears under-wear. Your father wears underwear!

BABYDOLL: Yes but he wears pants too!

HANCE: Big deal!. . .You don't seem to understand, Babydoll. I'm doing this country a great service—

BABYDOLL: Oh you're such a dreamer, Hance. You're completely out of touch with reality.

HANCE: Me!? You're the one that changes every five minutes.

BABYDOLL: Yes, I suppose I have changed Hance. . .Maybe we should separate for a while, maybe even get a divorce.

HANCE: *(panics, throws himself at* BABYDOLL'S *feet)* Divorce! Oh! God! Oh! How awful! Oh! Babydoll! I can't bear it!

BABYDOLL: Stop snivelling Hance. The neighbors might hear you.

HANCE: The neighbors! Who cares! Babydoll, don't you love me? I'm your husband! Don't do this to me!

BABYDOLL: Oh, Hance, yes, of course I love you. I just want something more out of life than we've been getting. I mean what kind of social life do we have? Zero, absolute zero.

HANCE: I ask you to go out all the time.

BABYDOLL: Hance, people stare at us. It's embarrassing. You've been arrested dozens of times. Is wearing pants all that much to ask?

HANCE: But I've got my profession to think of, my career. I'm an artist, Babydoll, an artist!

BABYDOLL: You're a cute quack!

HANCE: AN ARTIST! *(stares off into space, strikes hypotic photographic pose.)*

BABYDOLL: Jesus, Hance, I'm so bored. Let's go out and get some Mexican tv dinners an' heat 'em up in the park, you know, kinda like it was when we first met. . . *(wistfully)*. . .You even wore pants then.

HANCE: *(looks dreamily over horizon)* You know, Babydoll, someday, thanks to innovative scientific development of modern underwear and the plans and dreams of futurist underwear man might not even have to wear pants! *(amazed)* Just think of that!

BABYDOLL: Oh Jeezus Hance.

HANCE: *(assumes extended intellectual guise)* Consider life in space, for example. Your basic most functional unit of attire in extraterrestrial exploration is naturally, obviously going to be underwear.

BABYDOLL: Yeah, but if you don't wear anything over it, how can it still be underwear?

HANCE: *(perplexed for a moment)* Just trust the industry, Babydoll. Those designers are professionals. They know what they're doing. . .I can see it now. Maybe I'll even get to model the new underwear in outer space. Lights. Photograph. Space. Stars. Planets. Galaxies.

BABYDOLL: There must be something wrong somewhere. This man makes good money. He's kind, considerate, loving. We live in a good neighborhood. I shop at the grocery store right down the street. There are tulips in our front yard, roses in the back. Why won't my husband wear pants?

HANCE: Whatever happened to the FLAME that once burned within you, Babydoll? Whatever happened to your spirit? What of the romance, the excitement, the enchantment? When I would come to your window late at night in my diamond midnight invitee briefs and recite Lord Byron upon the balcony?

BABYDOLL: *(dreamily)* Yes, the days were filled with rose petals and roller coasters.

HANCE: We were impulsive, frivolous, alive, free, wild, adventurous!

BABYDOLL: Oh the night! The night touches me so delicately—the moonlight, soft whispers, silhouettes of forms upon the water. . .I remember it all so well.

HANCE: See what I mean BD Baby—you haven't changed at all. You're still the same wistful, impetuous, hopelessly romantic little creature I married.

(They sing and dance.)

BABYDOLL: I'm his cute little Babydoll—

HANCE: And I'm her great big handsome Hance.

BABYDOLL *and* HANCE: We share the greatest love of all—

BABYDOLL: But on my Hance he don't wear no pants.

HANCE: *(spoken)* But BD a man's gotta make a living.

BABYDOLL: *(sings)* But oh my Hance he don't wear no pants.

HANCE: *(spoken)* Oh come on Babydoll gimme a break.

BABYDOLL: *(sung)* But oh my Hance he don't wear no pants.

(They turn and face away from each other, then turn and face each other.)

HANCE: *(sung)* My darling I shall love you the rest of my life.

BABYDOLL: *(sung)* Sir I am honored to be your wife.

HANCE: We shall be the world's greatest romance.

BABYDOLL: But oh my Gallant won't you put on your pants?

HANCE: *(stops dancing and singing, strikes photographic pose.)* Never!

BABYDOLL: Oh my Handsome won't you put on your pants?

HANCE: *(strikes photographic pose.)* I refuse!

BABYDOLL: Oh my Dashing won't you put on your pants?

HANCE: I've got my career to think of.

BABYDOLL: I think I'm gonna throw up.

HANCE: Quick! Go to the bathroom! Do it in the toilet!

BABYDOLL: Oh Hance cut it out—I'm not really sick—that's just a figure of speech.

HANCE: Oh.

BABYDOLL: Jesus. *(disgust)*

HANCE: Huh?

BABYDOLL: Oh nothing.

HANCE: Oh. . .How about a little Lord Byron, Babydoll? Wouldn't you like to hear a little Lord Byron?

(Babydoll is silent, examining her fingernails. HANCE *strikes poetic pose.)*

HANCE: "She walks in beauty like the night of cloudless climes and starry skies and all that's best of dark and bright. . .(can't remember). . .and that's the best of dark and bright. . .oh shit.

BABYDOLL: *(laughs)* Serenading your wife with half a poem and in your underwear! You may be dumb, dumb, dumb, but sometimes you're kinda cute, cute, cute. *(kisses him, pinches his butt.)*

HANCE: It's not funny Babydoll! And I'm not dumb! I'm—*(assumes photographic pose)* an ARTIST!

BABYDOLL: You're a pretentious package of pudding in polka dot panties!

HANCE: An ARTIST! *(rapidly assumes several different photographic poses)*

BABYDOLL: You're an alleyway Andy with an anxious angle.

HANCE: Artist! . . .Artist want cookie!

(BABYDOLL exits. Bag of cookies flies thru the room. HANCE retrieves it. Begins eating cookies. BD returns.)

HANCE: Artist want cigar!

(BABYDOLL exits, returns with big cigar, sticks it in HANCE'S mouth, lights it. HANCE continues to eat cookies.)

HANCE: Artist want beer!

(BABYDOLL exits, returns with beer, HANCE begins to drink beer while eating cookies and smoking cigar. BD is coy and nonchalant.)

HANCE: What's for dinner, Babydoll? *(Sits down, watches tv.)*

BABYDOLL: Oh Hance let's go out to one of those Fun Pizza places where they play banjos and rinky tink pianos and everyone yells and sings funny songs.

HANCE: Remember the last time we went there? They kicked me out.

BABYDOLL: Oh You—CREEP! You're hopeless! I try to humor you, but sometimes I just can't take it anymore! You're a lost cause!

HANCE: What are you talking about woman? I put a roof over your head. I feed you. I clothe you. I love you and care for you. That's reality for you.

BABYDOLL: But couldn't you just once do all that with your pants on?

(She turns away weeping, HANCE sees she is markedly upset, does not know how to deal with it, bumbles around a bit, finally assumes photographic pose.)

HANCE: "One shade the more one ray the less had half impaired the nameless grace, Which— *(consternated)* Which— *(softer volume, straining memory)* One shade the more one ray the less had half impaired the nameless grace, Which— *(frustrated, sits back down, eats cookies. drinks beer.)* I know whatcha mean, kid, go on an' have a good cry. All this glamour can even get a big old Babydoll down once in a while. The Lights. The Camera. The Photograph. The Photograph. The Photograph. *(eats cookies, drinking beer, smokes cigars.)* "One shade the more one ray the less had half impaired the nameless grace, Which—— Oh shit, where is that book. *(exits.)*

(Enter MR. *and* MRS. DOLL, BABYDOLL'S *parents. She is still visibly upset when she sees them.* MR. *and* MRS. DOLL *carry thick catalogues and are visibly upset.)*

BABYDOLL: Momma! Poppa!

(Enter HANCE *with book. He recites while* MR. *and* MRS. DOLL *carry on.)*

HANCE: "Which waves in every raven tress or softly lightens o'er her face Where thoughts serenely sweet express. How pure how dear their dwelling place. And o'er that cheek and on that brow so soft so calm yet eloquent. The smiles that win, the tints that glow, But tell of days in goodness spent, A mind at peace with all. A heart whose love is innocent!

MRS. DOLL: Oh God IT IS him! It's him! *(compares picture to* HANCE*)*

MR. DOLL: Eureka Martha! It is! It is!

MRS. DOLL: Oh! Oh! Married! To our daughter! Him! Oh! I'm going to faint!

MR. DOLL: Martha!

BABYDOLL: Mother!

HANCE: Good evening Mr. Doll. Good evening Mrs. Doll. Lovely weather don't you think? Do you enjoy Lord Byron?

BABYDOLL: Here, Daddy, let's put her on the couch.

(They lift her onto couch or chair. MR. DOLL *lightly slaps her cheeks.)*

MR. DOLL: All right there, Okay. That's it Martha.

BABYDOLL: Would you like some coffee Momma?

MRS. DOLL: I need a drink. Get me a drink!

HANCE: How about a beer? It's all we got.

MRS. DOLL: Anything. Anything.

HANCE: How about you, Mr. Doll?

MR. DOLL: Yes Yes.

(exit HANCE.*)*

MR. DOLL: Feel better now, dear?

MRS. DOLL: I need a drink.

BABYDOLL: Mother, I can explain everything.

MR. DOLL: You can't explain anything, young lady. It's plain to see that you're married to—to—to—an, "UNDERWEAR MODELER!!!"

(Enter HANCE *with four beers on a tray.)*

HANCE: And what the hell is wrong with that? I'm a professional man. I've got my integrity to think of. I'm an artist!

MRS. DOLL: *(chugs beer)* You're a disgrace to our daughter! You're a perverted punk!

MR. DOLL: *(chugs beer)* You're a sleazy snake in the subway of humanity!

BABYDOLL: He's a cute clown, but Jesus, if you would only wear pants, Hance. *(drinks beer)*

HANCE: Professional discretion! I'm an artist! Artist! Artist! *(drinks beer)*

MRS. DOLL: *(chugs beer)* You're a wimpish weasel—

MR. DOLL: *(chugs beer)* A wayward witch of the underwear world!

HANCE: I'm a celebrity, a man with a future. *(drinks beer)*

MRS. DOLL: *(chugs beer, laughs)* You're a dangerous dog with a fever in your fern!

MR. DOLL: *(chugs beer, laughs)* You're a wretched runt, a psychotic spectacle!

BABYDOLL: Quit it! He's my husband and I know he's a jerk but he's my husband and I love him. I wish he would wear pants but he's my husband and I love him. But Hance, for God's sakes won't you PLEASEPUTONSOMEPANTS!!!

HANCE: *(assumes photographic pose)* Never.

MRS. DOLL: I need another beer! *(Throws empty can across room.)*

HANCE: Righto my dear. Four more cold ones coming up. *(Jumps in air, clicks his heels, exits.)*

MR. DOLL: You know, he may be a creep, but you've got to admit the boy's got spirit. I like to see a boy with some spirit, a young fella with some spunk.

MRS. DOLL: And all this time we thought he was a travelling meat buyer—don't hig legs ever get cold?

BABYDOLL: He's really very dedicated Mother.

MRS. DOLL: Dedicated to what, I dare ask?

HANCE: *(enters with 4 beers on tray, strikes several photographic poses, delivers beers.)* To my Art!

MR. DOLL: Well tell, Hance, just what kind of future is there for a young man in the—uh, in the—uh, the "underwear modeling" business?

HANCE: Unlimited, Mr. Doll, Unlimited.

MR. DOLL: Well, I mean, how much could a really top notch, uh—underwear modeler expect to make? *(guzzles beer)*

HANCE: Let's put it this way, Mr. Doll. If you're a star, you make a star's wages, right? So the sky's the limit. The sky's the limit.

MR. DOLL: I see. Hmmmmnn. *(guzzles beer.)*

MRS. DOLL: *(guzzles beer)* Well you certainly have a nice place here. I'll admit that much.

BABYDOLL: Oh thank you Mother.

MR. DOLL: Well, I mean, what are the possibilities for advancement in this line? What's the future hold in store for the uh, the underwear modeling industry?

HANCE: This business is just about to bust wide open, Mr. Doll. Modern civilization is preparing to move into a revolutionary new Age of Underwear. Underwear will become the initial motivating phenomenon of our daily lives as well as our long range intentions. Underwear is basic, primary, universal. Many cultures today are returning to their roots, as the sociologists like to say.

MRS. DOLL: *(guzzles beer)* Babydoll, where did you GET this guy?

MR. DOLL: Oh do continue. Do continue.

HANCE: *(guzzles beer)* Well you see it's all so terribly logical, terribly solid—One might even say essential—wouldn't you agree?

MR. DOLL: *(guzzles beer)* Oh yes essential. Essential.

MRS. DOLL: Now don't you get mixed up in anything Chester. *(chugs beer)*

MR. DOLL: It's all right Martha, it's all right. We're all adults here. I think we can deal with this thing in a rational adult manner. Do continue. Do continue, uh— "son." *(guzzles beer)*

HANCE: *(sentimental and inspired)* Essential, yes, essential, logical, solid. . .*(pops elastic on his trunks)*. . .I like to think of underwear modeling as a meet the people job. In fact, I feel a warm sense of personal kinship with each and every individual who has my catalogues at home and sees me represented there in Living Color showing off a pair of—oh, say, Camouflage Colored Trail and Jungle Briefs. It's really an exciting field, Mr. Doll, really wide open.

MR. DOLL: Yes, yes, exciting, yes, I know what you mean, wide open. *(drinks beer)* uh, son.

MRS. DOLL: *(chugs beer)* Now you be careful, Chester. Don't you start talkin' crazy. This thing ain't just sick he's Slick! *(drinks beer)*

MR. DOLL: Just in the name of science Martha, just in the name of science. Do continue. Do continue. *(drinks beer,* BD *watches tv)*

HANCE: Yes—well, as I was saying, Mr. Doll, humanity has only begun to scratch the surface of the increasingly important underwear frontier—for example, I was telling Babydoll just tonight about the startling new innovations involving underwear in the exploration of outer space. You see, not only is underwear very functional and basic in today's world, but *(very inspired and prophetic)* it is also the Clothing of the Future!

MRS. DOLL: *(chugs beer)* Babydoll, WHERE did you GET this guy?

BABYDOLL: *(absorbed in tv, drinks beer)* Mmmmnnhhn.

MR. DOLL: Yeah, Hance, that really sounds interesting. I think I'm beginning to see what you mean. *(drinks beer)*

MRS. DOLL: Chester! Don't be ridiculous! *(drinks beer)*

MR. DOLL: In the name of science Martha in the name of science. Progress. *(drinks beer)*

HANCE: And do you know what's gonna be right in there at the focal point of the latter 20th century technological progress, Mr. Doll? *(drinks beer)*

MR. DOLL: No! Whazat?!!?

HANCE: Underwear!

MR. DOLL: Ohmigod!

MRS. DOLL: Ohmigod! *(disgusted, bored)*

HANCE: You may think that the oil shortage is a bad thing, folks, but just wait till we have an underwear shortage! That's gonna be a real crisis!

MRS. DOLL: *(guzzling beer)* Oh! Hance! Is there going to be a sh—sh—sh—shortage??!!??

HANCE: Maybe. Maybe. You never can tell. That's why it's so important that we use our resources wisely.

MRS. DOLL: *(queasy and nervous)* Oh—my— I need another beer.

MR. DOLL: Me too Hance. Me too.

BABYDOLL: I'll get it. *(exits)*

MR. DOLL: Well, Hance, do you think we oughta—stock up, you know?

HANCE: No. No, don't think so. Might create a panic, you know. Gotta play it cool.Yeah. Play it cool.

MR. DOLL: Right. Play it cool.

MRS. DOLL: Play it cool. Right.

HANCE: And that's where the importance of underwear modeling comes in, by helping maintain a constant awareness in the public's mind of the essential fundamental stature of underwear.

BABYDOLL: *(enters with a tray of beers)* Oh Hance you've got such a way with words. You should go into politics. But I think you'd have to wear pants.

HANCE: *(strikes photographic pose)* Oh I don't know Babydoll, I think the public might vote for a man in a pair of red, white, and blue "OLD GLORY" jockies. *(strikes photographic pose)* But actually I feel as though I'm more needed in the underwear modeling field. *(strikes photographic pose, toasts with his beer)* PHOTOGRAPH BABYDOLL!!!

BABYDOLL: *(drinks beer, toasts)* PHOTOGRAPH! OH! PHOTOGRAPH!

MR. DOLL: *(seized with inspiration, takes his pants off)* PHOTOGRAPH! PHOTOGRAPH! *(toasts, drinks beer)*

BABYDOLL: OH! HANCE! OH! PHOTOGRAPH!

MRS. DOLL: Photograph? *(guzzles beer)*

18

BABYDOLL: PHOTOGRAPH! OH! OH LIGHTS! OH CAMERA! OH! HANCE! OH! PHOTOGRAPH! OH ECSTACY! OH SACRED PASSION! OH DIVINE! OH INFINITE PHOTOGRAPH! PHOTOGRAPH!

(HANCE and MR. DOLL *strike many photographic poses,* HANCE *smiles like a winning athlete, all drink beer)*

MR. DOLL: Photograph! Photograph!

BABYDOLL: Let's dance! Oh Hance! Let's dance! *(she turns up tv, she and* HANCE *begin to dance)*

MR. DOLL: Photograph. Photograph. Yes, Interesting. Er—eh—uh—Hey, Martha, let's dance!

MRS. DOLL: Dance? Dance? Why, Chester!

(MR. and MRS. DOLL *dance. Perhaps taped music is played, perhaps the four hum and sing. Dance transforms thru various styles, chosen by choreographer and/or performers. Dance reaches crescendo as the dancers spin off and proclaim their "Photographs" facing the audience as a large number of photographers appear popping flashbulbs.)*

MRS. DOLL: Photograph!

BABYDOLL: Photograph!

MR. DOLL: Photograph!

HANCE: Photograph!

ALL: PHOTOGRAPH! PHOTOGRAPH! PHOTOGRAPH!

(the four ad-lib as they leave the stage.)

Titles by Wings Press:

Robert Bonazzi, *Fictive Music*
Susan Bright, *julia*
Judson Crews, *Nolo Contendere*
Eleanor Earle Crockett, *'53 Ford*
M.W. McGee, *Ambrosia Dancing at Mary's*
Vassar Miller, *Approaching Nada*
Vassar Miller, *Small Change*
David Plumb, *The Music Stopped
    and Your Monkey's On Fire*
Townes Van Zandt, *For the Sake of the Song*
Michael Ventura, *The Mollyhawk Poems*
A.D. Winans, *Venus in Pisces*

Wings Press
P.O. Box 25296
Houston, TX 77005